# Walking with Christ

DESIGN FOR DISCIPLESHIP

## DFD**3**

**NAVPRESS**

Discipleship Inside Out®

### NAVPRESS ⬤
#### Discipleship Inside Out®

NavPress is the publishing ministry of The Navigators, an international Christian organization and leader in personal spiritual development. NavPress is committed to helping people grow spiritually and enjoy lives of meaning and hope through personal and group resources that are biblically rooted, culturally relevant, and highly practical.

**For a free catalog go to www.NavPress.com**
**or call 1.800.366.7788 in the United States or 1.800.839.4769 in Canada.**

ISBN 978-1-60006-006-9

Cover design by Arvid Wallen
Cover illustration by Michael Halbert
Interior design by The DesignWorks Group
Creative Team: Dan Rich, Kathy Mosier, Arvid Wallen, Pamela Poll, Pat Reinheimer,
    Kathy Guist

Original DFD Author: Chuck Broughton
Revision Team: Dennis Stokes, Judy Gomoll, Christine Weddle, Ralph Ennis

Printed in the United States of America

9 10 11 12 13 14 / 18 17 16 15 14 13

# DFD3 | CONTENTS

# GETTING THE MOST FROM YOUR STUDY

The Bible is a book of life, a treasure chest of truth for living life well. Psalm 19:7-11 tells us that the Bible

- *Refreshes the soul*
- *Makes the simple wise*
- *Gives joy to the heart*
- *Gives light to the eyes*
- *Is more precious than gold*
- *Is sweeter than honey*
- *Yields great reward when we obey its teachings*

God has provided abundant wisdom and riches in His Word, which are available to every believer. But only those who seek diligently will experience them. An open heart, meditation, and prayer are three keys that will unlock this storehouse of God's wisdom as you study. As you look up the verses in this study, take time to meditate on them prayerfully. This will help you understand their meaning and live them out in your life.

In *Walking with Christ*, you will study five important aspects of your life with Him:

- *Maturing in Christ*
- *The Lordship of Christ*
- *Faith and the Promises of God*
- *Knowing God's Will*
- *Walking As a Servant*

# 1

# Maturing in Christ

Today's world is flooded with inventions that meet people's needs quickly and easily: instant foods, instant communication, instant information available on the Internet. We must remember, however, that there is no such thing as "instant maturity" in following Jesus. Becoming a believer begins a lifelong adventure of knowing God better, loving Him more, and being transformed into the likeness of Christ.

> Don't become so well-adjusted to your culture that you fit into it without even thinking. Instead, fix your attention on God. You'll be changed from the inside out. Readily recognize what he wants from you, and quickly respond to it. Unlike the culture around you, always dragging you down to its level of immaturity, God brings the best out of you, develops well-formed maturity in you. (Romans 12:2, MSG)

1. Read Colossians 2:6-7. How did you begin your life in Christ?

   How should you continue to grow?

2. Consider Romans 5:1-5. Because of your justification by faith in Christ, what practical benefits are yours to experience?

Why can this give you hope?

3. Read Ephesians 1:1-14 and list several things you have as a result of being in Christ.

4. You took your first step toward spiritual maturity when you put your faith in Christ. Record here the important points of the gospel message you believed, including scriptural references for each.

5. Read Ephesians 4:11-16.

   a. What is God's desire for you? (verses 13,15)

   b. What are some characteristics of immature believers ("children" or "infants")? (verse 14)

   c. According to this passage, what characterizes a spiritually mature person?

   d. What part can others play in our maturing? (See also Hebrews 3:13 and Ephesians 5:19-21)

6. Contrast man's old nature with the believer's new nature. (Ephesians 4:22-24)

| Old Nature | New Nature |
|---|---|
|  |  |

7. Consider 2 Corinthians 3:18.

   a. Into whose image are you being changed?

   b. Who brings about this change?

   c. Are you completely changed all at once? Explain.

8. What do the following verses in Romans tell you about your relationship to Christ?

a. What has already happened to you? (5:8-9)

b. What should you be doing now? (6:19)

c. What can you expect in the future? (8:16-18)

Three aspects of salvation in Christ are helpful in understanding God's plan for believers:

| Justification | *Past* tense—I have been saved . . . from the penalty of sin. | My *position* is in Christ. |
|---|---|---|
| Sanctification/ Transformation | *Present* tense—I am being saved . . . from the power of sin. | My *condition* is becoming like Christ. |
| Glorification | *Future* tense—I will be saved . . . from the presence of sin. | My *expectation* is to be like Christ. |

When you look at your salvation — past, present, and future — how does this give you hope?

9. Think carefully about Colossians 3:2-4. How do these verses relate to the preceding chart?

## THE PROCESS OF GROWTH

10. There are many similarities between physical life and spiritual life. What do you learn about these similarities from the following verses?

1 Thessalonians 2:11

1 Timothy 4:8

1 Peter 2:2-3

From your experience or observation, what is another similarity between physical growth and spiritual growth?

11. Meditate on Romans 6:11-13.

    a. What should you count as true about yourself? (verse 11)

    b. What should be your present relationship to sin? (verse 12)

    c. What must you not allow? (verse 13)

    d. What action should you take? (verse 13)

    e. How would you explain the truth of Romans 6:5-6 in your own words?

12. God intends for you to reign in life (Romans 5:17), not for sin to reign in your life (Romans 6:12). What application do these verses suggest for your life?

13. Paul stated that believers are saved through faith (Ephesians 2:8-9), but your relationship to God does not end there.

a. According to Ephesians 2:10, what are you?

b. What did He create you to do?

c. What is God doing now? (Philippians 1:6)

d. What is one particular area of your life where you sense God has been working recently?

> **"** What would it mean, I ask myself, if I too came to the place where I saw my primary identity in life as "the one Jesus loves"? How differently would I view myself at the end of the day?
>
> —Philip Yancey, *What's So Amazing About Grace?*

O ur outer person is merely God's frame — the real picture is the inner person that God, the Artist, is still creating. As you reflect on your life, be thankful for all that God is doing in you. Conflicts in your life should encourage you because they indicate that God is still working in you, changing you to be like Christ. Take a moment to express your gratitude to God for what He has done, is doing, and will do for you.

## HOW TO LIVE

14. Using 1 John 1:6-10, contrast those who walk in fellowship with God and those who do not.

| People in Fellowship with God | People Not in Fellowship with God |
|---|---|
|  |  |
|  |  |
|  |  |
|  |  |

15. Read Hebrews 5:13-14.

    a. What is a mark of a mature believer?

    b. In what ways do you encounter good and evil in your daily life?

    c. When you face evil, do you usually desire that judgment or mercy will triumph? (James 2:12-13)

> The mature Christians I have met along the way are those who have failed and have learned to live gracefully with their failure. Faithfulness requires the courage to risk everything on Jesus, the willingness to keep growing, and the readiness to risk failure throughout our lives.
>
> —Brennan Manning, *Reflections for Ragamuffins*

16. What attitude should mature followers of Jesus possess?
    (Philippians 3:13-15)

17. Read 1 Corinthians 15:58. While
    awaiting eternity with Christ, what
    should believers be doing?

What assurance from this verse can motivate you to do this?

18. What are some areas in which you can experience spiritual
    growth?

    1 Timothy 4:12

    2 Peter 3:18

1 John 4:16-17

19. Toward the end of his life, Paul wrote a letter to Timothy, his son in the faith. Read 2 Timothy 4:7-8. What statement was Paul able to make concerning his earthly walk with Christ?

What did he expectantly await in the future?

**Colossians 2:7**

Rooted and built up in him, strengthened in the faith as you were taught, and overflowing with thankfulness.

**Colossians 2:7**

**MY JOURNAL**

How have you matured in Christ over the past six months or so?

► God intends followers of Jesus to mature and become like Christ. God has saved His children from the penalty of sin. While on earth, they struggle with sin, but they can anticipate a sinless future with Christ as glorified beings.

► Faith in Jesus Christ marks the beginning of spiritual growth. Believers have God's resources available to help them grow.

► Spiritual growth is similar to physical growth. It takes time as God works in believers' lives. Believers should reign in life, recognizing that God is bringing to fulfillment the work He began in them.

► Growing in Christ is similar to walking. Led by the Spirit, followers of Jesus are to walk in faith, in love, and in fellowship with Christ.

► A mature believer is one who continues to follow Christ, faithfully serving Christ and experiencing His grace and love. God does not forget the work of the believer and will one day reward him.

## GOING DEEPER

List the names of several believers you know personally and view as spiritually mature. Call, e-mail, or visit one of these people. Ask these questions and record his or her answers in the space that follows:

What has God used to mature you?

What have you learned during your journey toward spiritual maturity?

Other questions?

# 2

# The Lordship of Christ

Jesus Christ is both Savior and Lord—not just the Lord of His followers but also the Lord of all lords. Not all people presently acknowledge Him as their Lord, but that does not alter the fact of His lordship. Someday in eternity, every single person will be forced to acknowledge Christ as Lord. Until then, anyone who is willing to trust Him totally has the privilege of coming under Christ's influence and obeying His lordship. Christ becomes our Lord first by a decision made through trust and then by the daily practice of willing obedience. Under the leadership of Jesus, we can have complete confidence in His loving protection.

# THE LORD JESUS CHRIST

1. Titles reveal important information about the person to whom they refer. What are Jesus Christ's titles in the following verses?

   John 13:13

   Acts 2:36

   Revelation 19:16

   Summarize what these titles reveal about Jesus Christ.

2. Jesus Christ is Lord of what and whom? (Connect the following answers with the corresponding references.)

   |  |  |
   |---|---|
   | Creation | Colossians 1:16-17 |
   | The living and the dead | Colossians 1:18 |
   | All believers—the church | Romans 14:9 |

3. Write your own definition of the word *Lord* as you feel it applies to Jesus Christ. (A dictionary may be helpful in giving you some ideas.)

4. Read Philippians 2:9-11.

   a. How has God exalted Jesus Christ?

   b. How will every person exalt Him?

5. How do the angels acknowledge Christ's lordship in Revelation 5:11-12?

6. Read 1 Corinthians 6:19-20.

   a. How did you become God's possession?


   b. Because of this, what should you do?


   c. How do you feel about being God's possession?

## ACKNOWLEDGE HIS LORDSHIP BY DECISION

Christ should have the same place in our hearts that He holds in the universe.


7. What place should Jesus hold in a believer's life?
   (Colossians 1:18)

What would it look like for Christ to hold the same place in your heart that He holds in the universe?

8. What are we commanded to do in Romans 12:1?

Why should we do this?

9. Of the following sentences, check any that you would use to complete this phrase: I generally think or feel that . . .

\_\_\_\_ Jesus doesn't really understand my problems.

\_\_\_\_ He may want me to do something I can't.

\_\_\_\_ He may want me to enter a career that I would not enjoy.

\_\_\_\_ He has already let me down.

\_\_\_\_ He will prevent me from getting married.

___ He will take away my enjoyment of possessions, hobbies, or friends.

___ He can help me in the big things, but He doesn't care about the little things.

What other fears or emotions have prevented you from giving Christ access to every area of your life?

How does the revealing of God's heart in Jeremiah 29:11 dispel these fears?

10. Consider this quote comparing lordship to a marriage covenant. What similarities do you see between a bride giving herself to her groom in loving, lifelong trust and believers giving themselves to Christ in loving, lifelong trust, for better or for worse?

A clear and definite activity of the will is involved in recognizing his lordship, since he is to be Lord of all. By her "I will" the bride at the marriage altar, ideally, forever enthrones her groom in her affections. In subsequent years she lives out in detail all that was implied in that momentary act of the will. A similar enthronement of Christ can result from a similar act of the will, for the same decision as enthrones Christ automatically dethrones self.

— J. Oswald Sanders*

a. What, if anything, thrills you about surrendering to Christ that way?

b. What, if anything, frightens you about that kind of all-or-nothing surrender to Christ's lordship?

---

* J. Oswald Sanders, *The Pursuit of the Holy* (Grand Rapids, MI: Zondervan, 1972), 65.

11. Consider the following questions and check the appropriate box.

|  | Me | Jesus |
| --- | --- | --- |
| Who knows perfectly what is best for my life? | ☐ | ☐ |
| Who is most able to do what is best for my life? | ☐ | ☐ |
| Who desires at all times what is truly best for my life? | ☐ | ☐ |

Even though we know how good God is, why do you think it is still so hard to surrender control of our lives?

12. What has God given us to help us trust Christ and obey Him as our Lord? (2 Peter 1:3-4)

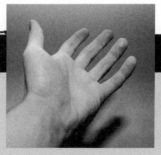

## PRAYER PAUSE

Pause for a while to pray over the place Jesus holds in your heart. Tell Him how you feel about abandoning yourself to His authority and trusting His lordship over every aspect of your life. Admit any fears you have and let Him hear your commitment as well.

Good intentions don't guarantee good results. A good start does not ensure a strong finish. Decision is only the beginning. Once you have decided to acknowledge the lordship of Christ in your life, you will prove that He is Lord by submitting to Him hour by hour and obeying Him in the daily affairs of life, such as those represented in the following illustration.

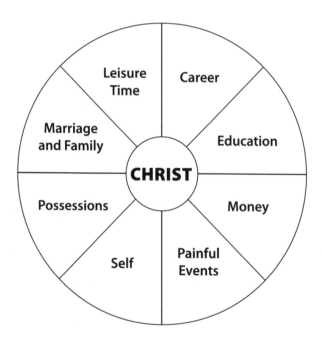

13. Take a few moments to evaluate your surrender to the lordship of Jesus Christ in each one of these areas. A good way to determine if Christ is in control is to ask yourself, "Am I willing to do whatever Christ desires in this area?" or "Will I be able to thank God for whatever may happen in this area?"

a. Which areas in the illustration, if any, are you not allowing Christ to control?


b. Are there other areas not mentioned on the chart that you are not allowing Jesus to control? Explain what they are and why you hesitate to trust Jesus' authority in those areas.


c. What can you do in these areas to invite Christ's lordship?

We should not be concerned about what we would do for the Lord if we only had more money, time, or education. Instead, we must decide what we will do with the things we have now. What really matters is not who or what we are but whether Christ controls us.


14. Whenever you assume control of your life, you will soon become unhappy and anxious. What did Peter say you can do? (1 Peter 5:6-7)

15. What can happen if cares and worries are not committed to Jesus? (Mark 4:18-19)

How do you think this takes place?

16. In Luke 9:23, what three things is a follower of Christ called to do? (Write them in your own words.)

17. According to Luke 6:46, what is a good way to evaluate if Jesus is truly Lord of your life?

18. Read Luke 18:28-30.

a. What had the apostles done?

b. What did Jesus promise to those who follow Him as Lord?

c. Describe a particular time or situation when you obeyed this command. What was the effect on you and others?

19. How does Christ exercise His loving protection and lordship over His followers? (Ephesians 5:24-27)

20. What does the lordship of Christ mean to you personally?

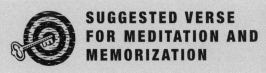 

**Colossians 1:16**

For in him all things were created: things in heaven and on earth, visible and invisible, whether thrones or powers or rulers or authorities; all things have been created through him and for him.

**Colossians 1:16**

It takes real humility to admit that Jesus has even better plans for your life than you do. It takes deep trust to actually give Him the reins of your life and invite Him to live through you. Consider the following quote. Journal about where you are currently in your willingness to follow Him as your Lord.

> It is to the Lord Jesus that you abandon yourself.
> It is also the Lord whom you will follow as the Way;
> It is this Lord that you will hear as the Truth, and it is from this Lord that you will receive Life.
> If you follow Him as the Way, you will hear Him as the Truth and He will bring life to you as the Life.

— Jean Guyon

► Jesus Christ is declared to be Lord in the Scriptures. He is worthy to be Lord because of who He is and what He has done.

► Because Jesus Christ is Lord, the believer's responsibility is to acknowledge His authority every day in all areas of his life.

► Various areas of a believer's life may not be subject to the control of Christ. The follower of Jesus should submit these areas to Christ and continue to recognize that Christ's control of his life is for his own welfare and joy.

Meditate on each verse in Colossians 1:13-22. In the chart that follows, summarize in your own words what each verse says is true about the Lord Jesus or about you as His follower.

| Verse | True About the Lord Jesus | True About Me |
|-------|---------------------------|---------------|
| 13 | | |
| 14 | | |
| 15 | | |
| 16 | | |
| 17 | | |
| 18 | | |
| 19 | | |
| 20 | | |
| 21 | | |
| 22 | | |

How do these truths and assurances from God's Word affect your willingness to surrender joyfully to His lordship in your life?

# 3

# Faith and the Promises of God

**A**group of people once asked Jesus how they could do the work of God. Jesus replied, "The work of God is this: to believe in the one he has sent" (John 6:29). God desires belief and faith from us, for "without faith it is impossible to please God" (Hebrews 11:6).

But often our faith is nothing more than wishful thinking — "I hope everything works out all right. I have faith that it will." The biblical concept of faith far surpasses this superficial approach. Biblical faith says, "Lord, I trust You!"

1. What part does our faith play in beginning to walk with God? (Ephesians 2:8-9)

   Having received Christ by faith, how should you now live? (Colossians 2:6)

2. How would you define faith according to the following verses?

   Acts 27:25

   Romans 4:20-21

   Hebrews 11:1

> **❝** Faith is the assurance that the thing which God has said in his word is true, and that God will act according to what he has said in his word. . . . Faith is not a matter of impressions, nor of probabilities, nor of appearances.
>
> —George Muller, quoted in *George Muller: Man of Faith and Miracles*

3. What does faith make possible? Match the following.

| | |
|---|---|
| ___ hope, joy, peace | a. Matthew 21:22 |
| ___ answered prayer | b. James 2:23 |
| ___ power over Satan | c. Ephesians 3:12 |
| ___ access to God | d. Ephesians 6:16 |
| ___ intimacy with God | e. Romans 15:13 |

Real faith moves from belief in what is true *about* God to a trusting intimacy *with* God.

4. State the principle of 2 Corinthians 5:7 in your own words. Then give an example of how you can live out this truth in your daily life.

5. What sin can exclude you from seeing God work? (Matthew 13:58)

> The opposite of faith is not doubt; it is unbelief. Doubt only needs more facts. Unbelief is disobedience and refuses to act in accordance with what God has declared.
>
> — Adaptation of Reverend Charles G. Finney, *Systematic Theology*

6. Read the story of Thomas's struggles with doubt in John 20:24-29. How did Jesus respond to his doubts?

How do you expect Jesus to respond to you in your times of doubt?

> Faith in God is a relationship involving all of who you are and all that is around you. Faith is a lived encounter, a relationship of truth with the divine.
>
> —Leonard Sweet, *Out of the Question . . . Into the Mystery: Getting Lost in the GodLife Relationship*

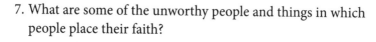

## OBJECTS OF FAITH

7. What are some of the unworthy people and things in which people place their faith?

   Psalm 33:16-17

   Psalm 146:3

   Proverbs 3:5

   Proverbs 28:26

   Jeremiah 9:23-24

Place a check by those you find yourself most likely to depend on. What do you think is the inevitable result of placing faith in these people and things?

8. Who should be the object of your faith? (Mark 11:22)

9. Your confidence and faith in God are built on your knowledge of who God is and what He is like. What verses about God's nature and character have been significant to you?

| Verse | What This Shows Me About God |
|---|---|
|  |  |
|  |  |
|  |  |
|  |  |
|  |  |
|  |  |
|  |  |
|  |  |

10. Hebrews 11 is a key chapter on faith. Read through the entire chapter, taking note of the many things accomplished by faith.

  a. Which of the things accomplished by faith do you consider to be the most significant? Why?

  b. How do you think God deepened the faith of the people mentioned in Hebrews 11? (Notice especially verses 9,17,25,34,37-38.)

  c. Many of the people in Hebrews 11 waited years — or a lifetime — before seeing God fulfill His promise. What happens to your faith when God asks you to wait?

> God delights to increase the faith of His children. . . . I say—and say it deliberately—trials, obstacles, difficulties, and sometimes defeats, are the very food of faith.
>
> —Miles J. Stanford, *Principles of Spiritual Growth*

## THE PROMISES OF GOD

11. Think of a specific time when someone promised you something.

    a. How did you evaluate whether or not this person would keep his or her promise?

    b. Did he or she keep it?

    c. How does this affect your attitude toward his or her future promises?

12. God also makes certain promises to you. What does Scripture say about the words of God?

    1 Kings 8:56

    Psalm 89:34

Isaiah 55:11

2 Peter 1:4

13. Why do you think God's promises are trustworthy?

## PROMISES TO CLAIM

14. Fill in the following chart.

| Verses | Promise | Condition |
|---|---|---|
| John 15:7 | | |
| Lamentations 3:22-26 | | |
| Romans 8:28 | | |

15. Why do you think God places conditions on some promises?

16. What is God's attitude about fulfilling His promises to you? (2 Corinthians 1:20)

17. Read Hebrews 6:12,16-19.

    a. What should your attitude be in claiming God's promises? (verse 12)

    b. Why do people make promises and swear oaths to one another? (verse 16)

c. Why did God make promises to His children?
(verses 17-19)

It is helpful and encouraging to note God's promises. You may want to keep a list of these promises, their conditions, and their results. God's promises often form a "chain" like the examples below.

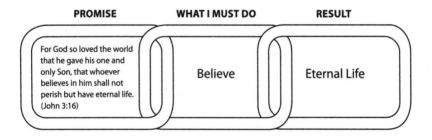

PROMISE — WHAT I MUST DO — RESULT

For God so loved the world that he gave his one and only Son, that whoever believes in him shall not perish but have eternal life. (John 3:16)

Believe

Eternal Life

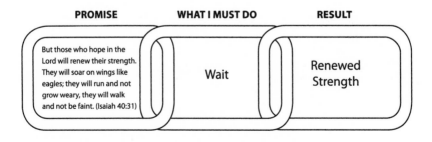

PROMISE — WHAT I MUST DO — RESULT

But those who hope in the Lord will renew their strength. They will soar on wings like eagles; they will run and not grow weary, they will walk and not be faint. (Isaiah 40:31)

Wait

Renewed Strength

18. Discover how Jehoshaphat utilized the promises of God. Read 2 Chronicles 20:1-30.

a. What was the first thing Jehoshaphat did? (verses 3,6-12)

b. How did God answer him? (verse 15)

c. Was this a promise?

d. What was Jehoshaphat's next response? (verse 18)

e. What evidence is there that Jehoshaphat believed God's promise?

f. How did he encourage others? (verse 20)

g. What was the result? (verses 22,27)

19. What is one promise you have discovered in your Bible reading?

Specifically, how has this promise helped you?

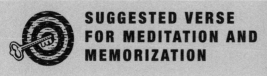

**Hebrews 11:6**

And without faith it is impossible to please God, because anyone who comes to him must believe that he exists and that he rewards those who earnestly seek him.

**Hebrews 11:6**

How have you seen God fulfill His promises to you?

What have you promised God?

Are you trustworthy to Him?

**POINTS TO REMEMBER**

▶ Faith is based on the fact that God is trustworthy to keep His word and fulfill every one of His promises.

▶ People may entrust their lives to a number of things that will ultimately fail. The only worthy object of faith is God.

▶ God's words never fail. God always does what He says he will do because He is faithful to His word.

▶ Believers should claim God's promises because He desires to respond to our faith.

God did a great thing to restore the people in Israel during the time of Nehemiah. This brought a great expression of faith from the Levites and other leaders, as expressed in Nehemiah 9.

Through the eyes of faith they pointed to some wonderful things about God, the object of their faith. In the first twenty verses, the people praised God for being:

- *Glorious (verse 5)*
- *Unique, exclusive (verse 6)*
- *Creator, bringing something out of nothing (verse 6)*
- *Life-giving (verse 6)*
- *Worthy of praise (verse 6)*
- *Sovereign, in control (verse 7)*
- *Deliverer (verse 7)*
- *The name changer (verse 7)*
- *Promise keeper (verse 8)*
- *Righteous (verse 8)*
- *Aware of pain (verse 9)*
- *Wonder worker, able to change anything (verse 10)*
- *Helper and leader (verse 12)*
- *Fair and just law giver (verse 13)*
- *Provider (verse 15)*
- *Gracious, compassionate, forgiving (verse 17)*
- *Faithful guide (verse 19)*
- *Never abandoning (verse 19)*
- *Teacher (verse 20)*

Meditate on Nehemiah 9:21-27. Add other words or phrases that describe God.

## PRAYER PAUSE

Use this list to lead you into a time of worship and praise to God. Thank Him for all the reasons you have to trust Him completely.

# 4

# Knowing God's Will

Sometimes it may seem to you that God's will is hidden behind a locked door. But is this true? Is God keeping His plans from you as some hidden secret? Or will He allow you to follow Him, leading you step by step?

Proverbs 3:5-6 encourages,

> Trust in the LORD with all your heart
>     and lean not on your own understanding;
> in all your ways submit to him,
>     and he will make your paths straight.

The key to knowing God's will is understanding His heart for you and developing a good relationship with Him.

> The will of God is not like a magic package let down from heaven by a string. The will of God is far more like a scroll that unrolls every day. . . . The will of God is something to be discerned and to be lived out every day of our lives. It is not something to be grasped as a package once for all. Our call, therefore, is basically not to follow a plan or a blueprint, or to go to a place or take up a work, but rather to follow the Lord Jesus Christ.
>
> —Paul Little, *Affirming the Will of God*

## THE REVEALED WILL OF GOD

1. What should one of your desires be as a follower of Christ? (Ephesians 5:17)

2. What does God promise you concerning His will for your life, and what does this reveal about His heart for you? (Psalm 32:8)

3. What does God reveal about His will for you in the following verses?

1 Thessalonians 4:3 (Sanctified means "set aside for holy purposes.")

1 Thessalonians 5:18

4. What was the psalmist's attitude toward God's will in Psalm 40:8?

What actions help produce this attitude? (see also Psalm 40:10)

5. Who is your source of strength to do God's will?

John 15:5

Philippians 2:13

We often face decisions on issues that the Scriptures do not provide specific instructions for. In these cases, a follower of Jesus should apply the principles of decision making that are contained in Scripture.

## PRINCIPLES OF DECISION MAKING

People have tried many methods to determine what God wants them to do.

- *Fleeces (asking God for a supernatural sign)*
- *Fasting (giving up food to seek out God)*
- *Flipping coins (leaving it up to the toss)*
- *Feeling (obeying only their feelings)*
- *Floundering (fishing everywhere for answers)*
- *Defaulting (letting events decide)*
- *Dipping (reading random Bible passages)*
- *Delegating (letting others decide for them)*
- *Dreaming (asking for a vision or a voice)*
- *Sitting (procrastinating)*
- *Sliding (taking the course of least resistance)*
- *Thinking (using logic in spite of feelings)\**

6. Which of these, if any, have you tried? What was the result?

---

\* *How Can I Know What God Wants Me to Do?* Radio Bible Class Publication (Grand Rapids, MI, 1987), 3.

## GOALS FROM SCRIPTURE

God has given particular commandments that can help you make decisions concerning your activities. If a particular course of action is inconsistent with the Bible, then you know it is not His will for you.

7. Using the following verses, express in your own words some of God's objectives for you.

    Matthew 6:33

    Matthew 22:37-39

    2 Corinthians 5:20

    1 Peter 1:15

    2 Peter 3:18

Ask yourself the following questions based on these and similar verses to determine your course of action:

- *Am I putting God's desire ahead of my own?*
- *Will this help me love God and others more?*
- *Will this help me fulfill the Great Commission?*
- *Will this help me lead a more holy and compassionate life?*
- *Will this increase my intimacy with and worship of God?*

Answering these questions honestly will help you make a decision in accordance with God's Word.

8. Using the following verses, develop your own questions that will help you discern God's will.

1 Corinthians 6:12

1 Corinthians 6:19-20

1 Corinthians 8:9

1 Corinthians 10:31

Galatians 6:7-8

Following Jesus is more like a pathway than a tightrope. We need to follow the ways of Jesus — love, humility, honoring the Father — and listen to Him in prayer for specific guidance. Sometimes God is silent: As a Father He wants us to grow through decision making. Sometimes God is very directive: He guides us through His Word with the help of the Holy Spirit. In this manner, we grow to be strong-willed, submitted people who honor and love God and serve others in humility.

## OBEDIENCE TO GOD

If you refuse to obey God in what He has already shown you, why should He give you further direction? Obedience to the known will of God is important in receiving additional guidance.

9. How do you gain an understanding of God's will?

Psalm 37:31

Psalm 119:105,130

10. What else can you do to understand God's will?

Psalm 143:8

James 1:5

11. Psalm 25:4-5 is a prayer of David concerning God's direction for his life. Write this prayer in your own words and use it as a prayer for yourself if it reflects your own heart.

12. What conditions for finding God's will are given in Romans 12:1-2?

13. What will the Holy Spirit do as you seek direction from God? (John 16:13)

14. Read Isaiah 30:18. Why do you think the Lord sometimes wants you to wait before He reveals His will to you?

## OPENNESS TO GOD'S LEADING

Many difficulties in determining the Lord's will are overcome when you are truly ready to do whatever His will may be.

15. You may not always know all the possible alternatives in determining what to do. What is a means by which you can gather additional information? (Proverbs 15:22)

Counsel should be obtained from mature believers who are committed to the will of God and who know you well. It helps to talk with others who have previously made decisions in matters you are presently experiencing.

16. Explain the principle Jesus used in answering those who were questioning Him. (John 7:17)

How does this apply to knowing God's will?

17. When you know what God wants you to do, how should you do it? (Ephesians 6:6)

18. What are other factors that can help you discern God's leading?

Romans 13:1

Ephesians 5:15-17

Colossians 3:15

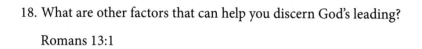 As we have seen, Christ's call means that we are to come after Him. The essence of that call involves the direction of our lives.

—Dr. Joseph Stowell, *Following Christ*

## PRINCIPLES IN PRACTICE

The following chart may be helpful in determining God's will for a particular decision you now face.

Decision I am facing:

| Scriptural Objectives | Yes | No | Neutral |
|---|---|---|---|
| Am I putting God's desire ahead of my own? | | | |
| Will this help me love God and others more? | | | |
| Will this help me fulfill the Great Commission? | | | |
| Will this help me lead a more holy and compassionate life? | | | |
| Will this increase my intimacy with and worship of God? | | | |
| Other questions: | | | |

## OBEDIENCE TO GOD

19. What have I seen recently in the Scriptures that relates to this decision?

20. Have I prayed about this decision?

## OPENNESS TO GOD'S LEADING

21. What are the various options I have in making this decision?

| Options | Advantages | Disadvantages |
| --- | --- | --- |
| | | |

22. Am I truly willing to do whatever God wants me to do?

23. What counsel have I received from others?

24. What false desires might I have?

25. What fears do I have about the way God might lead me?

26. With what decision do I feel inner spiritual peace?

27. What circumstances relate to this decision?

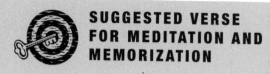

## SUGGESTED VERSE FOR MEDITATION AND MEMORIZATION

**Philippians 2:13**

For it is God who works in you to will and to act in order to fulfill his good purpose.

**Philippians 2:13**

Let's go back to Jeremiah 29:11 and Ephesians 2:10. Based on God's love, goodness, and desires for you, what are your hopes for the future? What do you think is the good work God may have prepared for you to do?

**POINTS TO REMEMBER**

▶ God has clearly revealed His purposes, values, and goals for us.

▶ In making decisions, seeking God above our own wants is necessary to discern God's specific desires for us.

▶ A willingness and openness to follow God comes before discovering a specific path.

▶ Asking good questions (such as those in this chapter) as we come before God is a helpful process.

**Option A:** During Jeremiah's time, God allowed the pagan King Nebuchadnezzar to conquer his people and take them to Babylon as captives. They struggled to understand how exile could be God's will for them. Read God's explanation of His will in Jeremiah 29:4-14.

a. How long were they to wait before God would rescue them? (verse 10)

b. In the meantime, how were they told to live? (verses 5-7)

c. How did God describe His plan and will for them? (verse 11)

d. What did God promise them if they would seek Him? (verses 12-14)

e. What do you discover about God's will from this story?

**Option B:** God's Will Illustration

The following illustration is not a formula for deciding God's will in specific situations. Rather, it illustrates areas to consider.

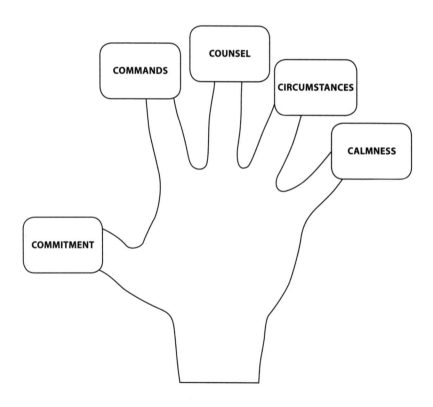

1. *COMMITMENT*—*Romans 12:1*
   - *Commitment not only to Christ's Lordship but also to what He will reveal as His path. We cannot say, "God, show me Your will, and if I like it, I will do it." (see Luke 6:46: "Why do you call me, 'Lord, Lord,' and do not do what I say?")*
2. *COMMANDS (God's Word reveals His will)*—*Psalm 119:105*
   - *Precepts that clearly state His will in many situations*
   - *Principles that show God's value system and approach*
   - *Promises in Scripture that offer direction in some instances*
3. *COUNSEL*—*Proverbs 12:15; 15:22*
   - *Someone speaking into your life and you speaking into the life of another; gaining and giving trust*
   - *Guards against "blindness," subjectivity, and oversight*
   - *Guidelines on seeking counsel:*
     a. *The person*
        - *Capable in the area of your decision*
        - *Demonstrates a heart for God*
        - *Somewhat or very familiar with you*
     b. *The process: Do not "shop around" in order to find counsel that agrees with you*
     c. *The product: Do not make a decision based only on what someone else says*
4. *CIRCUMSTANCES*—*Philippians 1:12-13*
   - *When God closed doors for Paul, other doors always opened. But an open door is not necessarily God's will just because it is open.*
   - *Providential circumstances are provided by God at His discretion. We cannot back God into a corner by requiring Him to clarify His will through circumstances.*
   - *God has given Satan limited control over circumstances (Job 1–2). The key for discerning which circumstances are from God is to follow closely to Him.*
   - *This includes how God created you: your gifts, abilities, and heart burdens. He wants you to live based on His unique design for you.*
5. *CALMNESS*—*Colossians 3:15*
   - *In praying over issues, there can be an inner sense of calmness regarding what is best.*
   - *Must be based on an assurance that God is leading, not on fleshly desire for an easy path to walk or on fleshly appeal (Proverbs 3:5-6)*

# 5

# Walking As a Servant

Everyone enjoys being served, but few enjoy making the effort to serve others. People often don't mind being called servants, but they do mind being treated as servants. Mature followers of Jesus are marked by what they will do for others without expecting anything in return.

## CHRIST YOUR EXAMPLE

1. What was Christ's purpose in coming to this world? (Mark 10:45)

What are some ways in which Jesus served people? (Matthew 9:35)

> To a world convinced that gain was measured in the accumulation of things, He said, "What good will it be for someone to gain the whole world, yet forfeit their soul?" (Matthew 16:26). Christ taught that the way to gain something is to give it away. The key to living is dying to self. Greatness is achieved through serving. Independence is not to be valued, but rather the submission of the follower, who then ultimately becomes useable, effective, and fulfilled.
>
> —Dr. Joseph Stowell, *Following Christ*

2. Read John 13:1-5,14-15.

    a. What simple act of service did Jesus do for His disciples? (verses 4-5)

    b. What gave Him the freedom and security to do this menial task? (verse 3)

    c. Why did He serve them this way? (verses 1,14-15)

    d. What are several lessons you learn from this passage?

3. Read Philippians 2:5-11.

    a. What did Christ give up, and what position did He take? (verses 6-7)

b. How did He demonstrate His servanthood? (verses 7-8)

c. Who do you think Jesus felt He was serving?

d. How and when did God reward Him for His humble service? (verses 8-11)

4. Consider that Jesus served even His betrayer. Who are the most difficult people for you to serve? How do you feel about serving them? What specifically can you do to serve them?

5. Reflect on God's instructions in Philippians 2:3-5.

   a. What are you told to do?

   b. How do you feel when you are treated like a servant? How do you deal with these emotions?

   c. Can you think of a situation in which you acted out of "selfish ambition or vain conceit" instead of valuing "others above yourselves"?

Pause to ask God where and whom He wants you to serve humbly, even though it may mean setting aside your own interests. Journal here on how He directs you.

6. From the passages in this chart, notice whom you should serve and any principles of service mentioned.

| Verses | Whom Should You Serve? | Principles About Serving |
|---|---|---|
| John 12:26 | | |
| Galatians 5:13 | | |
| Galatians 6:9-10 | | |

7. During Christ's last supper with the disciples before His death, He demonstrated several things about a serving attitude. Read Luke 22:24-27.

a. What were the disciples arguing about? (verse 24)

b. How should Christ's followers conduct themselves?
(verse 26)

c. How is this contrary to the way the world operates?
(verse 25)

> " The cause of Christ is empowered by fully devoted
> followers who get close to Him by seeing themselves
> as servants to others for the cause of eternity. We
> must never take for granted the reality that when
> the God of the universe became a man, He chose
> to come in the form of a servant (Phil. 2:5-11). It is
> a staggering thought that out of all the attributes
> He could have chosen, He chose humility so as to
> empower us toward growth and glory.
>
> —Dr. Joseph Stowell, *Following Christ*

Believers have been set free in Christ — not to do whatever they please, but to serve. Followers of Jesus are no longer under obligation to serve the things of the old life; rather, they are free to serve voluntarily the things of the new life.

8. According to the following Scripture passages, from what or whom did Jesus save us? What or whom can we now serve as a result?

| Verses | He Set Us Free From . . . | To Serve . . . |
|---|---|---|
| Romans 6:18-19 | | |
| 1 Peter 2:16 | | |
| Galatians 5:13 | | |

9. How did Paul see himself? (2 Corinthians 4:5)

How did he live out his identity as a servant?
(2 Corinthians 12:15)

## KEYS TO BEING A SERVANT

### BEING HUMBLE

10. What must you continually keep in mind? (John 13:13,16)

11. As a servant, you could develop pride in your serving. What can
    prevent that from happening? (Luke 17:10)

## OBSERVING AND MEETING THE NEEDS OF OTHERS

12. The servant is observant. "Ears that hear and eyes that see — the LORD has made them both" (Proverbs 20:12). God intends for you to use what He has given you to listen and observe.

    a. How could you become a better listener?

    b. How could you become a better observer?

13. What are some practical ways you could help meet others' needs? Proverbs 3:27

Matthew 25:35-36

1 John 3:17

14. With the previous question in mind, consider the following
people. How can you serve some of them this week?

- *Parents*
- *Siblings*
- *Friends*
- *Employers*
- *Teachers*
- *Employees*
- *Enemies*
- *Spiritual leaders*

## A SERVANT GIVES

One of the most tangible ways to serve others is to meet their material
and financial needs. If you are willing to give what is tangible, you will
be more likely to give what is intangible — your time, your experience,
your love, your life.

15. What principles and promises provide a foundation for New Testament giving?

2 Corinthians 8:9

2 Corinthians 9:6

2 Corinthians 9:8

Philippians 4:19

16. Our motivation for giving is very important. It isn't about obligation but rather a heart of worship and love. Consider John 12:1-7.

a. What was Mary's motive for giving?

b. What in general is your motive for giving?

c. If your motive isn't right, should that keep you from giving? Explain.

17. According to the verses in the following chart, to whom should you give? For each verse, can you think of a specific person to whom you could give?

| Verses | I Should Give To . . . | Specific Person I Can Give To . . . |
|---|---|---|
| Proverbs 19:17 | | |
| 1 Corinthians 9:14 | | |
| Galatians 6:6 | | |
| James 2:15-16 | | |

18. Evaluate your giving.

a. Do you have a plan?

b. To whom are you giving presently?

c. Do you need to change any of your giving practices? If so, what will you do?

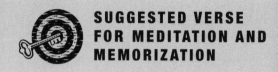

## SUGGESTED VERSE FOR MEDITATION AND MEMORIZATION

**Philippians 2:5-7**

In your relationships with one another, have the same mindset as Christ Jesus: Who, being in very nature God, did not consider equality with God something to be used to his own advantage, rather, he made himself nothing by taking the very nature of a servant, being made in human likeness.

**Philippians 2:5-7**

**MY JOURNAL**

How has Jesus served you this week? How have you served Him and others this week?

- Jesus Christ was not obligated to become a servant, but He did so voluntarily, giving of Himself to meet people's needs.

- Christ has helped all believers, and their response should be to serve Him and others.

- Believers must "die to self" in order to live for others. Then they are free to be servants.

- A servant must be humble and observant in little things as well as bigger ones.

- A server is a giver — not only of himself, but also of his material and financial possessions. Each believer should have a personal plan for financial giving based on scriptural principles.

God has given us spiritual gifts to serve others with love. Read about them in 1 Corinthians 12 and Romans 12:4-8. Which of these gifts might you have? How are you currently using or how might you use your spiritual gifts to serve other believers?

> The call to humility is a call to serve God with sober minds—with full awareness of our gifts and our limitations.
>
> —Gordon T. Smith

# THE ESSENTIAL BIBLE STUDY SERIES FOR TWENTY-FIRST-CENTURY FOLLOWERS OF CHRIST.

## DFD 1
**Your Life in Christ**                    978-1-60006-004-5
This concise, easy-to-follow Bible study reveals what it means to accept God's love for you, keep Christ at the center of your life, and live in the power of the Spirit.

## DFD 2
**The Spirit-Filled Follower of Jesus**                    978-1-60006-005-2
Learn what it means to be filled by the Spirit so that obedience, Bible study, prayer, fellowship, and witnessing become natural, meaningful aspects of your life.

## DFD 4
**The Character of a Follower of Jesus**                    978-1-60006-007-6
This insightful, easy-to-grasp Bible study helps you understand and put into action the internal qualities and values that should drive your life as a disciple of Christ.

## DFD 5
**Foundations for Faith**                    978-1-60006-008-3
This compelling Bible study will help you get a disciple's perspective on God, His Word, the Holy Spirit, spiritual warfare, and Christ's return.

## DFD 6
**Growing in Discipleship**                    978-1-60006-009-0
This study will provide insight and encouragement to help you grow as a true disciple of Christ by learning to share the blessings you've received from God.

## DFD 7
**Our Hope in Christ**                    978-1-60006-010-6
In this study of 1 Thessalonians, discover how to undertake a comprehensive analysis of a book of the Bible and gain effective Bible study principles that will last a lifetime.

## DFD Leader's Guide                    978-1-60006-011-3
The leader's guide provides all the insight and information needed to share the essential truths of discipleship with others, whether one-on-one or in small groups.

To order copies, call NavPress at 1-800-366-7788 or log on to www.navpress.com.

**NAVPRESS**

Discipleship Inside Out™